he says i'm fierce

poems by

Debbie Collins

Finishing Line Press
Georgetown, Kentucky

he says i'm fierce

ACKNOWLEDGMENTS

I am forever grateful to the following magazines and journals and their
editors for the original publishing of the following poems:

"Entertain Me" in *Anapest Journal*
"The Shouting Sun," "Please Leave," and "gonna kick tomorrow" in
antinarrative
"Complicit" in *Basil O'Flaherty*
"The Waltzing Fool" was placed with *The Blue Nib*
"Sweet Summer" in *Flatbush Review*
"He Says" and "The Collapse" in *Former People Journal*
"Upon Waking" in *Fourth and Sycamore*
"Mania" in Virginia Commonwealth University's *Medical Literary Messenger*
"The Attempt" in *Skin Literature*
"It's a Beautiful Day in the Neighborhood," "Disheveled," and "The Third
Saturday in June" in *Third Wednesday*
"Broken" in Weasel Press, *Voices for Peace*

Publisher: Leah Huete de Maines
Editor: Christen Kincaid
Cover Art: Bob Schnell, www.certaingravityphoto.com
Author Photo: Bob Schnell, www.certaingravityphoto.com
Cover Design: Elizabeth Maines McCleavy

Printed in the USA on acid-free paper.
Order online: www.finishinglinepress.com
also available on amazon.com

Author inquiries and mail orders:
Finishing Line Press
P. O. Box 1626
Georgetown, Kentucky 40324
U. S. A.

Table of Contents

for Jonathan

The Waltzing Fool

the neighbor has parked in my space again
and I am unreasonably pissed
but I'm afraid to say anything

his wife said he's been off his meds for weeks
then she moved out last Thursday

he strews furniture and pots and pans
across the lawn and into the street

there's a sofa cushion,
an ironing board, a ladle, a potted plant

I just don't know what to say
that won't sound like a cloud of lies

I'll leave him to his manic waltz
as he falls apart, piece by tiny piece,
surrounded by forks and knives and dirty sheets

Mania

My face is afire
Lit from within
By a brilliant madness
I want to harness this
Kinetic energy
For something useful
Like burning down
Buildings
Or felling
Trees
I'm alone in my head
Ready to release and
Relinquish
This terrible secret
Upon an unsuspecting world

The Attempt

the chalky protein shakes,
pink or chocolate
tasted like
failure to me
I'd slough them off
on the other crazies

the nurses threatened
to take my smokes away
if I didn't eat
but I liked the process
of whittling down,
baring bone

you brought me some,
not the brand I usually
smoked, but I was
touched nonetheless

we sat on my bed to talk
on the rough white sheets,
institutional and
reeking of bleach
they were an affront to me,
so clean

they found me with
sand in my hair,
sand in my mouth
on a beach in Laguna

I promised you
I would eat

Complicit

The spoon winks up at me,
its round face shining
with answers.
The needle speaks
of fire and waste.

You sometimes say
that I'm strongest
in my broken places.
I'm just broken now, not
strong. I am full of ruin.

I'll just have another hit and
lie some more, all the while
you're quiet in your grief.
You and your grief and your
awful silence.

gonna kick tomorrow

my life is full of light and I am righteous
in my suit of mirrors, so happy when
everything is so wrong

the habit, the habit

the god of pills is crouched down
in the corner of my room and he's
not leaving soon enough for you

the failing, the failure

you, on the edge of the bed with
my quick love in your hands
you can't look at me now

I'll try again tomorrow

He Says

I am fierce

He says I'm fierce

With my hair on fire and slash of a grin
Destroying all his good intentions

His hands write a song on my body
The lyrics thrum like jazz, alive in a smoky room

I devastate his jutting hip bones and
Sharp shins as he falls apart above me

I wake to find his face
A regrettable blur against the pillow

I make a pot of coffee and drink it all myself

He thinks I'm terribly beautiful

He says I'm fierce

The Third Saturday in June

I was nursing some cheap gin
at this depressing little celebration,

watching my ex-lover
kiss his simpering new wife,

her mouth puckered
like an anus.

Pity? No thanks,
I've got plenty, tangled

in her veil and in
his laugh.

More gin for me, the averted eyes
around me small and mean.

I sneak outside with my drink.
The silence never sounded better.

Disheveled

You've reduced me to
Wearing my bedroom slippers
To the grocery store

Is it noon yet?
Must be somewhere
The bourbon is calling my name

The ashtray is overflowing
And I am overwhelmed
By your leaving

I don't know when
I slipped your mind
And became irrelevant

I guess I'll go now
The bourbon is calling my name

Entertain Me

I was at the bar, nursing
a martini of broken men.
I was getting good at it.

I saw you talking to a girl in red
and decided to steal you away. When I did,
the red of her dress shrieked at me,
each sequin a glittering judgement.

I had you by the wrist, pulling you
across the party floor and out a door
flanked by huge pots of flowers.
The sweet peas and orchids were
wilted and forlorn.

The outside air hit us with the force of
a furnace, August born. "What now," you said.

Saturday Night Scotch

when I enter the church of your
arms and lips and beautiful eyes

I'm always wary of the
drunken stories and old excuses

you couldn't fit your key
in the lock again, I hoped the
neighbors didn't hear me plead

>   *please don't fall*

I couldn't love you more
but you make it so goddamn
hard some days

I just keep telling myself—
arms and sweet lips and beautiful eyes

Broken

every word a sharp rebuke
every tender blow a bruise
you stained my lips
strawberry red
and I tasted it
with the tip of my tongue

our friend's averted eyes
were all too telling

I couldn't love you more
until the battles
with tangled words
and clenched fists

became ordinary
became normal

leaving made me less for a while
but I am not there to disappoint you now

you were my sweet disaster
my beautiful broken man

The Downpour

the raindrops fall fat on
the yard, now shorn and
waiting for more sun while

the line of forgotten laundry
snaps in the wind, sheets and
underwear flapping with damp regret

I unfold myself from my lawn chair
and listen for you, I thought
I heard you in the stillness

the awful weight of our words
spoken what seems like years ago
now pour down around me

just as the rain quickens and soaks
my head and our sheets, I wait
for the inevitable thunder
that I know will rumble inside

such a good boy

as we argued over the avocados, you said you loved me;
you think you do but it's only because I'm broken and you're a fixer

we have to be careful with each other, people say that
if you and I fall, we might not make it back up

my heart is always a wound for you to worry about
and I cry for us all the time

meanwhile, in the produce section of the grocery store,
as we set ourselves on fire in front of the tomatoes,

a service dog nibbles at the lettuce hanging over the side of the display—
the stuff was eye level, after all

Sweet Summer

The possibility of
a sweet, sweet summer

Seeps around the
edges of the blinds

Don't wake me
  you said

I bent to your lips
trying to rouse you
and tasted myself

I waited for you before
letting the sun crash in
through the windows now thrown open

Would you wake
If I promised you heaven?

I can make it happen
Love me

Please Leave

The sky is in a hurry,
rain beginning to rush from
swollen clouds. The stars
won't come out,
not tonight. By morning you'll
be gone and I'll wonder why
I even cared.

Upon Waking

The sunshine hurts my head
as I crab out of the bed
and onto the floor

The sheets trail behind me
like a widow's train
darkling and somber

All I can think about are
the always and nevers
and shouldn'ts and couldn'ts
that litter the floor

You've got your back to me
in naked reproach
and your shoulder blades
berate me

I draw the blinds and
ease back into bed
and pull you to me

You don't resist in your sleep
and I wish it could be so easy
to stay this way
beautifully awake

Jonathan

I had slept with a bouquet
of beautiful men but
you said you didn't care.

You petitioned my body
under a pale moon
as it slid between
hurrying clouds.

Your eyes were a riot
of blue that night.
Say something, I said, and
you said my name. Turns out
it was all I ever wanted.

The Shouting Sun

The spring downpour startles
the dogwood and camellia

and causes them to
scatter their brilliant blooms,

while the grass is acid
green and in desperate

need of cutting. I have
no motivation to move

as the pollen collects
in yellow drifts and clogs
my head and my thoughts.

I can't wait for summer,
heat baking the yard
and crisping tender leaves,

sunshine raining down,
glorious in its ruin.

Oh how I love the shouting sun.

It's a Beautiful Day in the Neighborhood
(Won't You Be Mine)

I'm the wife who smokes
and drinks too much and
peppers her conversations
with cuss words loud enough
for the kids to hear

I'm the wife who wears the obnoxious fringed
pants to the neighborhood cookout
and studiously ignores the sun-dressed
mothers with their ever-increasing herds,
kids galloping and shrieking all the damn time

I'm the wife who still wears college
jeans with holes in the knees
as the other wives order jogging tights
all the while eating mouthful after mouthful
of Julie's fabulous French-onion dip

I'm the wife who hates the cookouts
and Christmas parties and cocktail hours,
who hates the SUVs and
the manicured yards and the strollers

I could kick your kids at any second
and steal your husband with a look
I'm the bad wife of the neighborhood
I am chaos waiting to happen

The Collapse

the ivy is ever growing
up the mossy front of
our house

we get sun from the east
but a big sassafras
blocks it out as you slowly
do the same with me

all my gardener friends
tell me that the ivy will
creep in and work its way
into the mortar between the bricks

the house is crumbling around me
but I can't raise my head to care
let the ivy take over the ruin
of our house and our expectations

A native of Virginia, **Debbie Collins** writes from Richmond, where she studied English at Virginia Commonwealth University in the heart of the city. Richmond provides the backdrop for many of her poems.

Debbie's poetry has been published in many online and print journals including *Third Wednesday* and *The Wild Word*, and in the anthology *Lingering in the Margins*. She is a member of James River Writers and River City Poets. Debbie lives with her husband Jonathan in Richmond's Northside, where they let their dog Billy (the subject of many a haiku) drag them around the neighborhood on a daily basis.

CPSIA information can be obtained
at www.ICGtesting.com
Printed in the USA
BVHW040003060323
659725BV00035B/336